iPhone 14

USER GUIDE

The New Step-By-Step Manual For Beginners &
Seniors To Make The Most Out Of Your New
Smartphone. Complete & Easy Instructions To
Learn All Functions, Tips & Tricks And Much More.

Jeremy Plasner

Contents

INTRODUCTION:

In this book we will discuss about IPHONE and the total number of series that are already in market. IPHONE is widely used now a day, they are common and most importantly they are easily available everywhere. Whenever they launch a new IPHONE at first they are quite expensive only few can buy them still some people wait years for their new launch. Recently they are planning to launch IPHONE 14 PRO MAX on 7th of September 2022 and this will go on sale on 16th of September 2022 and pre-orders will begin from Friday 9th of September.

Before we will study about Iphone 14 we should know about the train of Iphones that are running from ages. Iphone is a line of a smartphones, they are designed and marketed by the APPLE company. They use Apple's IOS mobile operating system. This series of Iphone was first introduced and launched on January 9,2007 and then series is randomly generated over many years. This apple company kept releasing many models and keep updating IOS updates. Millions of Iphones are sold each year as people love their models so much. Iphones are designed for this modern world, many other companies also launch and produce their mobile phones but people always prefer IPHONES because they are advanced and best use for each and every day as they are advanced and being utilized in a specific and modern way. People also use IPHONES for a fashion purpose as they are fancy and quite expensive so having new launched iphone is also marked as a trend in a society.

At the Macworld convention on January 9, 2007, Apple co-founder Steve Jobs unveiled the first iPhone. Despite not being the first smartphone, the iPhone has helped the world's consumer and business populations transition to mobile computing. Its main competition has been Google Android-based handsets from manufacturers like Samsung, which were also released in 2007.

A selection of Apple programmes, including iTunes, Safari, and iPhoto, were preinstalled on the first-generation iPhone. Email services using Post Office Protocol 3 and Internet Message Access Protocol were integrated with the gadget. Although AT&T Wireless and Apple had an exclusive two-year distribution agreement for the iPhone, hackers managed to unlock the gadget in less than three months.

The second-generation iPhone and iPhone OS 2.0 were released by Apple on June 9, 2008. The name "iPhone 3G" was given to the new handset in reference to its new ability to connect to third-generation (3G) cellular networks, which are driven by technologies like the Universal Mobile Telecommunications System and high-speed downlink packet access (HSDPA). Eight and sixteen gigabyte variants of the iPhone 3G were offered.

Business-oriented features including support for Microsoft Exchange email were included in the iPhone OS 2.0 release. Secure access to business networks with Cisco's IPSec virtual private network was one of the newer mobile security features, along with remote wiping and other management options.

The IPHONES has a user interface that is built around a multi-touch screen. It also connects to cellular networks like WIFI so easily. They can be used to calls, message, video calls, we can easily use the internet can search anything from anywhere it's just like a high advanced models that can send and receive any mails. They are also use for entertainment, people watch, listens songs and movies. Many updates were available with time and age like they introduced big or larger screens, models were made water proof and as they can also install third party mobile apps through app store.

IPHONES are one of the two largest smartphone platforms in the world alongside Android, as they are forming the large part of the luxury market. These iphones generated so much profit for the apple company and making them one of the most valuable publicly traded companies. When IPHONES were first released they were known as first generation and described as revolutionary and a game changer for the mobile phone industry because they are so user friendly.

IPHONE comprises of both hardware and software where it contains most of the hardware parts of a typical modern smartphone hardware that are used in the creation of a model are 3D TOUCH, Taptic engine as they are unique to the Iphone. Many type of sensors are used for the touch screen such as proximity sensor, ambient light sensor, gyroscopic sensor, magnetometer, facial recognition sensor and most importantly finger print sensor. These all models of Iphones contains rear facing camera and front facing camera. From Iphone 7 series multiple lenses to the rear-facing camera was introduced.

If we talk about software's these all models run on operating system that are known as IOS and IPHONE OS it is also a variant of the Darvin operating system core found in macOS. These models of Iphones comes with a set of bundled applications developed by Apple. The best thing about these that Apple company provides free updates to the operating system for the IPHONE and majorly new updates have historically accompanied new models. If we discuss about the interface of the Iphones they are based around the home screen that's have a graphical list of available applications. For like all mobiles they also run one at a time. like others IPHONE all models contained the following apps like messages, calendars, photos, camera, YouTube, stocks, maps, weather, voice memo, notes, clock, calculator, settings.

Many models are updated and released up till now and hence they are famous and are widely used. Their applications and user friendly models made people so happy that they want to purchase their models at every cost. They recently launched IPHONE 14 and people are already over whelmed. Apple company is famous for their laptops like MACBOOKS, IPHONES as their new inventions are well needed in this market. People love their styles of models and their applications. Iphones are famous for their user friendly and for the advanced applications that are built in iphones and really important for daily routine. Many people think that IPHONES are waste of money as they are not pocket friendly and they require high maintenance plus they are expensive too. Still iphones aren't common in third world or un developed, developing countries due to high rise of prices of apple products. They are mostly common in developed countries like USA, UAE, CHINA as their people earn dollars and other great currencies so that they can easily purchase APPLE products.

IPHONE 13:

Apple Inc. conceived, produced, and marketed the iPhone 13 Pro and iPhone 13 Pro Max handsets. They are the flagship phones for the fifteenth generation of the iPhone, replacing the iPhone 12 Pro and iPhone 12 Pro Max. The smartphones were revealed alongside the iPhone 13 and iPhone 13 Mini at an Apple Special Event on September 14, 2021, at Apple Park in Cupertino, California, and went on sale 10 days later, on September 24. They, along with the iPhone 11 and iPhone 12 mini, were retired on September 7, 2022, following the unveiling of the iPhone 14 and iPhone 14 Pro. The iPhone 13 is offered in four different configurations, just as its predecessor: the iPhone 13, iPhone 13 small, iPhone 13 Pro, and iPhone 13 Pro Max.

On September 14, 2021, a virtual press event shot and recorded in Apple Park in Cupertino, California, officially unveiled the iPhone 13 Pro and iPhone 13 Pro Max together with the iPhone 13, iPhone 13 Mini, Apple Watch Series 7, 9th-generation iPad, and 6th-generation iPad Mini. Pre-orders went live at 5:00 AM PST on September 17. The iPhone 13 Pro and iPhone 13 Pro Max have similar starting prices as their respective prior models, at US$999 and US$1099, respectively.

The six-core A15 Bionic technology, which is exclusive to Apple, is incorporated into all iPhone 13 variants. Additionally, they enable Wi-Fi 6 (802.11ax) and Bluetooth 5.0 and contain a 5G chipset. All iPhone 13 versions have IP68 water resistance ratings, which indicate that a smartphone may function for up to 30 minutes in water up to 6 meters deep before becoming unusable. There are storage options of 128 GB, 256 GB, and 512 GB for all iPhone 13 models. With a maximum storage capacity of 1 TB, the iPhone 13 Pro Max is additionally available with the most space. With additional features that vary between models, the upgraded cameras on all iPhone models have been improved. A new cinematic mode, however, is supported by all models and automatically changes focus as a subject enters the frame. A 6.1-inch screen and a battery life of up to 19 hours of video playback are features of the entry-level iPhone 13 model. A smaller 5.4-inch screen and a battery life of only up to 17 hours are features of the iPhone 13 mini. Super Retina XDR displays and a two-camera system are shared by the base and small models. Both of them are equipped with twin 12MP wide- and ultra-wide-angle lenses.

The dual camera system has a 2x optical zoom and a 5x digital zoom. The iPhone 13 pro variants are a step up from the basic and mini, with pro features focusing on camera hardware upgrades. The iPhone 13 Pro has a 6.1-inch display, while the iPhone Pro Max has a 10% larger display at 6.7 inches. The display utilized in both pro models is the Super Retina XDR with ProMotion, which provides quicker screen refresh rates than the standard models. The usage of a three-camera system with telephoto, wide, and ultra-wide capabilities distinguishes the iPhone Pro. The pro camera system also features a higher optical zoom range than the base versions, measuring 6x, and a digital zoom of 15x. The iPhone 13 Pro cameras, like the iPhone 12 series, benefit from a LiDAR scanner for improved low-light and night photography.

The design of the iPhone 13 Pro and iPhone 13 Pro Max is nearly identical to that of their predecessors. However, thanks to the larger lenses, the back camera module now covers a greater area. The Face ID and camera module on the front display, or "notch," is now 20% smaller than in prior versions. The iPhone 13 Pro and 13 Pro Max are available in five different colours: silver, graphite, gold, sierra blue, and alpine green. Sierra Blue is a new hue that replaces Pacific Blue. On March 8, 2022, at Apple's Special Event "Peek Performance," Apple introduced a new Alpine Green colour option, which became available on March 18.

The hardware for IPHONE 13 is Apple created the A15 Bionic processor, which powers the iPhone 13 Pro and Pro Max. It has a 16-core neural engine, a 6-core CPU (with 2 speed cores and 4 efficiency cores), and a 5-core GPU. [23] Additionally, the A15 Bionic has a cutting-edge image processor. [Reference needed] In particular outside of the US, more 5G bands are accessible to support more carriers. The battery life of the iPhone 13 Pro and 13 Pro Max, according to Apple, is up to 1.5 hours longer than that of their respective predecessors. The iPhone 13 Pro's battery is rated at 11.97 Wh (3,095 mAh), up from the 10.78 Wh (2,815 mAh) battery found in the iPhone 12 Pro, while the iPhone 13 Pro Max's battery is rated at 16.75 Wh (4,352 mAh), up from the 14.13 Wh (3,687 mAh) battery found in the iPhone 12 Pro Max. [24] [25] Both devices include charging capabilities with MagSafe up to 15 W, Qi wireless charging up to 7.5 W, and Lightning up to 20–23 W for the (Pro), 20–27 W for the (Pro Max).

The iPhone 13 Pro has four cameras: a selfie camera on the front, a telephoto lens, a wide-angle lens, and an ultra-wide lens on the back. Compared to the iPhone 12 Pro, all of the rear-facing cameras have bigger sensors, which enable better light collection. To collect more light and improve performance in low light, the wide and ultra-wide also have wider apertures. Additionally, the ultra-wide camera now has focusing. Despite having a lower aperture than the 12 Pro's, the 77 mm telephoto offers the benefit of enabling Night Mode for the first time. The increased telephoto also boosts the digital zoom to a 15x range. Apple's most recent computational photography engine, known as Smart HDR 4, is utilized by the cameras.

The camera app now has a feature called Cinematic Mode that enables users to switch between topics while maintaining sharp focus by employing computer algorithms. It supports 1080p at 30 frames per second on wide, telephoto, and front-facing cameras. For devices with at least 256 GB of storage, Apple also included the option to record in Apple ProRes 4K at 30 fps and 1080p at 60 fps in iOS 15.1. Base models with 128 GB of storage will only be able to record in ProRes at 1080p at 30 fps. The camera has a macro setting that allows it to focus up to two centimeters away from a subject. It makes use of the ultra-wide camera's focusing and activates automatically when close enough to a subject.

IPHONE 14:

Apple Inc. created, created, and released the iPhone 14 and iPhone 14 Plus[a] handsets. On September 7, 2022, they were unveiled at the Apple Event in Apple Park in Cupertino, California, with the more expensive iPhone 14 Pro and iPhone 14 Pro Max flagships. They are the sixteenth generation of iPhones, succeeding the iPhone 13 and iPhone 13 Mini. The iPhone 14 and iPhone 14 Plus have improved rear-facing cameras, a 6.1-inch (15 cm) and 6.7-inch (17 cm) screens, and satellite connectivity. Launching with iOS 16, the iPhone 14 and iPhone 14 Plus will be released on September 16, 2022, and October 7, 2022, respectively. The iPhone 14 and iPhone 14 Plus are available for pre-order starting September 9, 2022.

The devices went on sale for the first time on September 16. Apple has four models this time around: the iPhone 14, 14 Plus, and 14 Pro Max. This version won't have a tiny model. All iPhone 14 versions come with storage options of 128 GB, 256 GB, 512 GB, and 1 TB. Only the 13 Pro Max model of the iPhone 13 had a 1 TB option. The A15 Bionic chip from Apple powers the iPhone 14 and 14 Plus, while the A16 Bionic chip, which is quicker, powers the 14 Pro and Max. Both devices have a 16-core neural engine, a five-core GPU, and a six-core CPU.

The iPhone 14 and 14 Max now provide a 6.1-inch display in place of the 5.4-inch small variant. Both the 14 Plus and the 14 Max Pro can expand to 6.7 inches in size. Apple's Super Retina XDR display provides a benefit to all iPhone 14 models. The Pro variants are brighter than the standard models, which have a maximum brightness of 1,200 nits.

With a redesigned front design that takes up less room for the camera notch at the top of the phone, the Pro models' form factors change slightly from those of the base versions. Apple also includes an always-on display feature with the Pro versions that is absent from the base devices. A new accelerometer, which Apple claims is better equipped to detect crashes and accidents, is also included in all iPhone 14 versions. Additionally, Apple has improved satellite connectivity for emergency services throughout the whole spectrum of iPhone 14 models.

The lesser 5.4-inch display size choice in the iPhone 14 series has been replaced by the new, larger 6.7-inch option. Since the release of the iPhone XS Max in 2018, the iPhone 14 Plus is the first less costly phablet iPhone model to see a price reduction. Since the iPhone 8 Plus in 2017, the "Plus" designation has not been used on an iPhone until the iPhone 14 Plus. The iPhone 14 and 14 Plus models, along with the iPhone 14 Pro and iPhone 14 Pro Max models, are the first iPhone models since the CDMA version of the iPhone 4 to not include a dedicated SIM card reader when they are sold in the United States.

Although the physical SIM tray is absent on the iPhone 14 and 14 Plus, both models and the iPhone 13 have the same design. There will be five colour options for the iPhone 14 and 14 Plus: Blue, Purple, Midnight, Starlight, and Product Red. Pink has made way for Purple as the new colour.

HARDWARE:

Chipset

The Apple A15 Bionic system on a chip, the same model as the iPhone 13 Pro and 13 Pro Max, is installed in the iPhone 14 and iPhone 14 Plus. The 6-core CPU, 5-core GPU, and 16-core Neural Engine of the iPhone 14 and 14 Plus.

Display

The 6.1-inch (15 cm) Super Retina XDR OLED display on the iPhone 14 has a refresh rate of 60 Hz, a resolution of 2532 x 1170 pixels, and a pixel density of around 460 PPI. The same technology is used in the 6.7-inch (17 cm) display of the iPhone 14 Plus, which has a pixel density of roughly 458 PPI and a resolution of 2780 x 1284 pixels. Each model has a maximum brightness of 1200 nits and a normal brightness of up to 800 nits.

Cameras

The iPhone 14 and 14 Plus have the same three-camera system, with a front-facing camera (12MP f/1.9) and two back-facing cameras (12MP f/1.5 wide and 12MP f/2.4 ultra-wide), both of which have quicker apertures than the iPhone 13's. Additionally, for the first time, the front-facing camera offers autofocus.

There are four models in Apple's new iPhone 14 series: the iPhone 14, iPhone 14 Plus, iPhone 14 Pro, and iPhone 14 Pro Max. Beginning on September 9, preorders for all of the phones will be accepted; the iPhone 14, iPhone 14 Pro, and iPhone 14 Pro Max are expected to ship on September 16. However, the iPhone 14 Plus won't be available until October 7th.

While maintaining Apple's A15 Bionic technology, the iPhone 14 and 14 Plus provide a number of upgrades to the iPhone series, including improved battery life and emergency messages via satellite. On the other hand, the more expensive iPhone 14 Pro and Pro Max also have the aforementioned satellite capability in addition to a new 48MP main camera, an always- The more expensive iPhone 14 Pro and Pro Max, which still have the aforementioned capabilities, include a larger display, as well as a notch replacement that shows notifications in real time.

The new A16 Bionic chip, which operates faster while using less energy than the prior generation chip, is one of many internal upgrades to the iPhone 14 Pro that can't be tested immediately. I quickly looked at the phone's camera, which now has a second 2x zoom option thanks to the upgraded 48-megapixel sensor in the primary camera (the iPhone 13 Pro also has a maximum 3x magnification, but the 2x zoom option is missing). I am aware that it is essentially a digital crop from a larger image, but it serves the purpose. The camera's other new features, including as the Action mode and Apple's new Photonic Engine image upgrades

MAIN DIFFERENCES BETWEEN THE 13 AND 14

Someone who is not familiar with Apple goods could find it difficult to distinguish many differences between the most recent iPhone and its predecessor. However, you can see how much the phone has changed over time by contrasting the iPhone 14 Pro with the iPhone XS. Only the most devoted iPhone users can recognise the updates in all their grandeur because the most recent iPhones always come with new and distinctive features. Learn more about how the iPhone 14 Pro differs from earlier models by reading on.

Is it worthwhile to upgrade to the newest model if you currently own the 13 Pro? To discover out, let's get into all the geeky and technical details!

Due to its smaller size, the recently released iPhone 14 Pro will be perfect for you if you don't feel like having a large phone in your pocket. But how does it vary from the iPhone 13 Pro from the prior year?

To help you decide whether it's time to upgrade, we've tallied up some of the significant differences between the iPhone 13 and the most recent iPhone 14. The Apple Watch Series 8, Apple Watch Ultra, and of course the newest iPhone 14 series were all unveiled during Apple's Far Out event. The 128GB version of the iPhone 14 will cost £849. The 256GB and 512GB editions will cost £959 and £1179, respectively. The 128GB, 256GB, and 512GB models of the iPhone 13 are identical and are available for £749, £859, and £1079 respectively. The four most important elements that you should be aware of if you want to compare the iPhone 14 to the iPhone 13 are listed below.

UPDATED CAMERA:

A new camera system has been added to the iPhone 14 with an emphasis on low-light performance and improved video stabilization. Additionally, it now has a wider sensor that is larger and has a faster f/1.5 aperture than the iPhone 13's f/1.6 aperture. The iPhone 14 is also the first iPhone to include auto-focus for the selfie camera, so your front-facing photos should have more detail and perform better in low light.

NO SIM CARD TRAY IN THE USA:

While not all customers will be affected, those who purchase the iPhone 14 in America will discover that it lacks a traditional SIM tray since Apple is encouraging users to use its new eSIM feature instead. The company introduced eSIM, enabling users to make calls and send texts without the need for a physical SIM, in collaboration with a number of mobile providers, including AT&T, TMobile, and Verizon. Users will also be able to install several eSIMs on a single device and install them without requiring an internet connection.

THE SAME A15 BIONIC CHIP:

The iPhone 14 will continue to use the same A15 Bionic chip that drives the iPhone 13, while being a part of the new line of smartphones. This implies that the performance of the iPhone 14 will be comparable to that of the iPhone 13 series, though we will be sure to validate these assertions once we receive devices for review. On the other hand, the newest

A16 Bionic chip, which is focused on power and efficiency, will be found in the iPhone 14 Pro and iPhone 14 Pro Max.

EMERGENCY SOS:

The iPhone 14 and iPhone 14 Plus also support Emergency SOS, allowing users who are unable to connect to the internet or data to connect their iPhone to satellite frequencies, allowing them to connect with emergency authorities if necessary. When in clear view of the sky, according to Apple, it can deliver a message in less than 15 seconds. Although Apple hasn't yet said how much it would cost after the first two years, this service is free during that period.

DIFFERENCE:

Apple appears to be addressing the one issue that would deter some customers from purchasing the Pro Max with the impending iPhone 14 Pro Max, namely its physical size With a smaller overall screen aspect ratio and a thinner screen border, the iPhone 14 Pro Max may have the same power as its bigger sibling but in a more user-friendly design. Apple is undoubtedly introducing its most advanced A16 Bionic chip, and a brand-new 48MP main camera is anticipated to dramatically improve image quality. But the total cost of all this could go up. Let's start with the distinctions between the iPhone 14 Pro Max and iPhone 13 Pro Max since those are the focus of this post.

Here are the key changes between the iPhone 14 Pro Max and iPhone 13 Pro Max:

- taller aspect ratio and thinner screen borders

- a punch hole in the form of a pill (dubbed the Dynamic Island), as opposed to a notch
- More rapid A16 Bionic chip
- constant-on display
- Satellite connectivity for a new 48MP primary camera

In summary, the iPhone 14 Pro appears to be a small improvement over the 13 Pro. Moreover, it is probably time to replace the older model based on what we have seen from Apple.

The iPhone 14 Pro is the most potent iPhone available right now, and because of its always-on display, enhanced low-light photography, and more effective processing, it has quickly risen to the top of our want list. With safety features like Crash Detection and Emergency SOS via satellite and a more potent A16 bionic chip, the primary camera sensor has been enlarged and brightened. Additionally, the new, thinner body of the 14 Pro is a subtle but essential upgrade that will make the phone seem more ergonomic for users who prefer smaller phones.

FEATURES OF IPHONE 14:

DESIGN AND DISPLAY QUALITY

The new 14 Pro Max will appear slightly smaller. The iPhone 14 Pro Max has the same flat sides, recognizable glass and stainless steel materials, same-sized screen, and overall design as its predecessor. The new 14 Pro Max's proportions, however, have changed. The phone will be thinner and simpler to hold in one hand due to the display's higher aspect ratio. But what you'll probably notice the most is the new, pill-shaped Face ID system that has taken the notch's place on the front. It takes up less room while giving the new iPhone 14 Pro series a unique appearance.

Another notable upgrade from the iPhone 13 Pro Max to the iPhone 14 Pro Max is the always-on display.

There are four different colour options available for the iPhone 14 Pro Max: deep purple, gold, silver, and space black. The iPhone 13 Pro Max is available in five colours: alpine green, silver, gold, graphite, and sierra blue.

The contents of the box, which will consist solely of a Lightning cord and no charger, are not expected to change. The 13 Pro Max features a 19.5:9 aspect ratio, whilst the iPhone 14 Pro Max has thinner screen boundaries and a taller, 20:9 aspect ratio. To improve outdoor viewing comfort, Apple has increased the 14 Pro Max's maximum brightness even higher (up to 2000 nits). Additionally, because they are both Pro models, they both include 120Hz ProMotion for incredibly smooth scrolling. Both employ Face ID for biometric purposes. The 14 Pro Max has the same sensors and face recognition technology as the 13 Pro Max, so the Face ID experience is the same despite the new pill design.

PERFORMANCE AND SOFTWARE:

The iPhone 14 Pro Max from Apple employs the new Apple A16 Bionic CPU, an improvement over the A15 chipset seen in the 13 Pro Max. It appears that issues will prohibit the iPhone 14 Pro from being Apple's first handset with a 3nm CPU, and the A16 will instead to be constructed using 4nm technology, a smaller step up from the 5nm process used on the 13 series.

Apple is maintaining the same 6GB of RAM on the 14 Pro Max as it did on the model before it. As anticipated, iOS 16 will make its debut on the iPhone 14 Pro Max. As usual, the 13 Pro Max will also receive the iOS 16 upgrade around the same time. Both of these devices are completely future-proof because Apple typically updates its phones every five or even six years.

CAMERA:

First, the main camera now has a larger 48-megapixel sensor, an improvement over the 12MP one from the previous iteration. Additionally, we anticipate enhancements to Cinematic Mode, a standout feature of the iPhone 13 Pro Max that blurs the background in videos just like Portrait Mode does for images. Apple was really proud of it, but there are still some bugs and the quality is just 1080p. The long-awaited periscope lens is one feature that won't be included on the iPhone 14 Pro Max. This year, iPhones won't be able to compete with native long-zoom lenses, which Android rivals like the Samsung Galaxy S22 Ultra have had for a while.

Differences between the 13 Pro Max and 14 Pro Max's official cameras:

Official camera changes between the iPhone 14 Pro Max and 13 Pro Max: 1X camera: 14 Pro Max has 48MP, whereas 13 Pro Max has 12MP. 12MP, f/2.2 on the 14 Pro Max, and 12MP, f/1.8 on the 13 Pro Max with the 0.5X camera. 12MP, f/2.8 on both 3x cameras.

AUDIO QUALITY AND HAPTICS:

Although we haven't heard anything in the rumor mill concerning sound quality upgrades, we keep our fingers crossed for the 14 series. The iPhone 13 series made a significant boost in audio quality with boomier, fuller sound on all three models.

Finally, keep in mind that neither device has a headphone port (and it's unlikely that it ever will). The Taptic Engine of the iPhone 13 Pro Max provided excellent haptic feedback, which we also found to be quite pleasing. So far, we anticipate that the 14 series will operate in the same manner.

BATTERY LIFE AND CHARGING:

The 14 Pro Max will be a battery beast even if it keeps its predecessor's longevity. The battery life on the iPhone 13 Pro Max has improved over its predecessor, in part because of the battery's larger physical capacity. Apple hasn't altered the iPhone 14 Pro Max's battery size this year, so it's likely to be the same.

- Size of the iPhone 14 Pro Max battery: 4,352 mAh
- Size of the iPhone 13 Pro Max battery: 4,352 mAh

No changes either on the charging front. When using a suitable charger, a complete top-up with the 13 Pro Max takes about two hours. This charger allows charging at 27W rates. On the more recent 14 Pro Max, we anticipate that things will be much the same. Both the iPhone 14 and 13 series are compatible with MagSafe, a magnetic wireless charging system with 15W of charging power.

SUMMARY:

In the end, Apple has so far been successful in keeping the iPhone 14 Pro Max intriguing. With the new pill-shaped Face ID cutout, the notch is finally eliminated, at least for the Pro iPhone models, along with a more potent A16 CPU and 48-megapixel main camera. The display size, 5G connection, A15 Bionic technology, and design of the iPhone 13 and iPhone 14 are identical. A further GPU core, satellite Emergency SOS, the Photonic Engine, and Action Mode are just a few of the advancements that the iPhone 14 still offers. The improvements of the iPhone 14 over the iPhone 13 are primarily incremental, including minor improvements to the camera and videography performance, battery life, and GPU. More important improvements for the safety-conscious include the upgraded camera hardware, 6GB of memory, and the three functions that are also included with the iPhone 14 Pro and iPhone 14 Pro Max: Crash Detection, Emergency SOS, and Satellite. Having said that, users upgrading from an earlier handset are probably best suited for the iPhone 14.

At first glance, there probably isn't enough to convince most users to choose the new model over the iPhone 13. In the event that you choose a larger display, things can be different. However, the iPhone 13 series does not offer an alternative to the iPhone 14 Plus. Since the iPhone 13 is still very functional for daily use and the iPhone 14 shares the majority of the features of the former, it might be preferable to wait for a more significant upgrade of the most adaptable features of the iPhone 13, such as the A15 Bionic chip, OLED

Super Retina XDR display, Ceramic Shield, Night mode, MagSafe, and IP68 water resistance.

FEATURES OF THE IOS INSTALLED ON IPHONE 14:

Every year (since the introduction of the original iPhone), new versions of the iOS operating system are published by Apple, adding new features and enhancing the user experience. It won't change with iOS 16 in 2022. iOS 16 will improve your iPhone with new features, like a configurable lock screen (complete with widgets), a reworked notification system, new Messages adjustments, and much more. It was first unveiled at WWDC 2022 back in June. The release of iOS 16 is scheduled for next week, as Apple announced at its iPhone 14 presentation, however not all iPhone users will be able to get the software. Everything you need to know about iOS 16—including its key features and anticipated release date.

With iOS 16, available on the iPhone 14 and iPhone 14 Plus, customers will experience iPhone in a new way thanks to a redesigned Lock Screen and new communication, sharing, and intelligence features. The Lock Screen is more appealing than ever because to a multilayered effect that deftly places photo topics in front of the time and newly created widgets that provide information quickly. They personalised, lovely, and practical than ever. The wallpaper gallery offers many options for Lock Screen inspiration, including Apple collections, a Weather wallpaper that enables users to view the current weather conditions as they change throughout the day, an Astronomy wallpaper that shows images of the Earth, moon, and solar system, among many other options.

Users can now edit or remember recently sent messages with and can unread discussions so you can go back to them later. Sharing a collection of images with relatives is now even simpler thanks to iCloud Shared Photo Library. In addition, Visual Look Up adds a new feature that enables users to tap and hold on an image's subject to lift it out of the background and place it in apps like Messages, giving Live Text more power by enabling it to recognise text in video, quickly convert currencies, translate text, and more. Live Text also gains the ability to recognise text in videos.

FEATURES IN IOS 16 THAT WILL BE INSTALLED ON IPHONE 14:

SYSTEM FEATURES:

1. Lockscreen:

Now that widgets are supported, the lock screen's appearance can be changed. The date and time's typeface and text colour can be changed, and colour effects can be used across the lock screen. A little widget can be put next to the date, which is now above the time. On the third row, beneath the time, more widgets may be inserted and positioned horizontally. There can be several lock screens set up. The live wallpapers are no longer present. Now that the phone is in landscape mode, the elements on the lock screen are arranged horizontally rather than vertically.

2. Improved focus mode:

Depending on the current focus, different lock screens can be configured. Apps can use focus filters to display various material depending on the active focus. For instance, the Mail app can only display email messages that don't originate from work contacts if they are not in the permitted list for Work, and Safari can only display active tabs that are work-related if the user is in the Work focus. In addition to lists of permitted apps and contacts, it is now also possible to construct lists of those that should be quiet.

3. Notifications:

Now, notifications can show up below the lock screen instead than above it. Notifications can be displayed in one of three ways: count, stack, or list. Two fingers can be used to group notifications to turn them into a counter. New lock screen notification widgets that display data in real time enable users to monitor events continually without being inundated with individual notifications. They benefit from the new Real-time Notifications iOS 16 introduced.

4. Control center:

In Control Center, a new drop-down menu displays all applications that have recently utilised the camera, microphone, or location. There is also a new toggle in Control Center for fast notes. Instead of being divided, the histories of the sound recognition Shazam function and the main Shazam programme are now integrated.

5. Status window

On select iPhones with Face ID (except iPhone XR, iPhone 11, iPhone 12 mini, and iPhone 13 mini), the battery level can now be seen in the status bar, saving the user from having to bring down the Control Center.

6. Settings in landscape

The Settings app now supports landscape mode, displaying the currently open setting page on the right and the setting list on the left.

7. Improved dictation

The keyboard is always available during text dictation, allowing the user to seamlessly move from speaking to manually typing and vice versa. Emojis can also be added or deleted via dictation. When there is a gap in the dictation, Auto-Punctuation automatically inserts a period.

8. Improved live text

The capacity to choose and edit text in videos is improved. Commands that can be executed instantly are known as quick actions. Text can be instantly translated or prices can be converted to another currency. Support was extended to include Ukrainian, Korean, and Japanese

9. Improving Visual Search

Visual Search can now distinguish people and objects in images, and it can interact with them by dragging and dropping them into other apps.

10. Siri advancements

Saying "Hey Siri, Hang-up" will end both FaceTime and cell phone calls. Now, Siri can play notifications over the speaker.

11. Spotlight

A new button that enables quick access to Spotlight from the Home Screen. To make it easier to use the phone with one hand, the search input text box is now fixed to the keyboard rather than being at the top. Apps like Messages, Notes, and

Files produce more image results. Such as launching a timer or executing a shortcut.

12. Translate

Now, the user can turn on the camera to translate any detected text in real time. Supports Dutch, Indonesian, Polish, Thai, Turkish, and Vietnamese in addition.

13. Improved accessibility

With the use of the camera's door detecting feature, blind persons can be directed. It can detect the presence of a door and signal how far it is away in terms of metres. The user can now lock their phone to prevent it from being used to end phone calls thanks to a new accessibility feature.

14. Network enhancements for Wi-Fi

Wi-Fi networks that have already been saved are now displayed and can be changed, removed, or selected to view the network password following Face ID or Touch ID login. Users have no other choice but to tap the settings app's "forget this network" button while connected to the network in question in order to disconnect from previously linked networks. Users might also choose "erase network settings" from Settings—>General->Transfer or reset iPhone (at bottom)->Reset->Reset Network Settings to completely remove all previously recognised networks from their iOS devices. The latter choice is commonly suggested to people who want to resolve a variety of Wi-Fi and cellular network issues that may arise on their iOS devices.

15. A Cell phone network upgrade:

The eSIM from another iPhone can be transferred via Bluetooth during Cellular Network setting.

16. Backups:

Along with 5G and Wi-Fi, 4G can now be used for iCloud backups.

17. Face ID:

The phone can now be held horizontally and still use Face ID. Only the iPhone 13 and soon-to-be-released iPhone 14 models are eligible.

18. Keyboard

Users have the option of turning on haptic feedback, which causes a slight vibration to be felt while they type, simulating the action of pressing mechanical keys.

19. Controller Support:

Joy-Con and Pro Controllers for the Nintendo Switch can now be connected with iOS 16, iPadOS 16, and tvOS 16.

20. Artificial Reality:

Using the LiDAR Scanner included with the iPhone 12 Pro and iPhone 12 Pro Max, a new framework called Room Plan will enable apps to swiftly build 3D floor plans of rooms.

APP FEATURES:

Some of the app features are:

1. Messages:

Sent messages include a 15-minute editing window and a 2-minute deletion window. the ability to label a conversation entirely as unread. The Messages app now has Share Play, which enables users to view a movie or listen to music with friends without having to initiate a FaceTime conversation. Deleted texts can be recovered for up to 30 days. Collaboration is the ability to enlist others in a project so that you are informed whenever someone makes changes to a shared document in a thread within the Messages app. It works with third-party apps created to take advantage of this Collaboration functionality as well as iOS apps including Files, Keynote, Numbers, Pages, Notes, Reminders, and Safari. Users can use their finger to precisely place themselves on the sound wave graph for previously transmitted or received audio communications. The ability to inform carriers about SMS/MMS trash.

2. Face Time:

What is spoken during a FaceTime call is automatically translated by FaceTime Live Captions.

3. MAIL:

It is possible to plan when to send messages with Mail. Within ten seconds, a newly sent email can be cancelled. Ability to move messages that the user hasn't responded to to the top of the list and create a reminder. Typos are corrected through improved search based on the messages they contain. Email communications now have additional context and details at a glance thanks to new rich links.

4. MAPS:

Maps now offers multi-stop routing. Routes can have as many as 15 stops total added as intermediate stops. While navigating, users may also ask Siri to create a new stop point. Pay in Transit now has a fare calculator. The Detailed City Experience and Look Around now support new Map Kit capabilities.

5. Photos:

The user's photo collection can be shared with up to five contacts. These contacts have complete control over editing and deleting shared photos. A new tool makes it possible for users to find duplicate photographs in albums.

Face ID or Touch ID are now required to access the Hidden and Recently Deleted albums.

The ability to replicate filters and effects from one image to another is now available.

You may look for specific words inside of photos.

There is now a Wallpaper format for cropping photographs that will crop the image to match the aspect ratio of the device's display.

Automatic duplication detection finds and gathers together duplicate images or videos.

The duplicates' pertinent data will be combined with the higher-quality version of the image, which will be maintained.

6. Camera:

The ability to choose whether a photo will be instantly posted to their shared photo library or solely stored to their personal photo library is toggled while capturing the picture.

The live translation function is embedded into the camera app's viewfinder.

7. Shared tab groups in Safari:

Users can collaborate on groups of tabs and see in real time which tabs others are currently viewing.

Pinned tabs: You can pin tabs to the top of the opened tabs display.

Start pages for tab groups: There may be a distinct start page for each tab group that includes Favorites, Frequently Visited, etc.

Extension syncing allows you to choose which extensions to install on your current device after viewing those that have already been set up on other devices. Simply enable them on one device, and they will be enabled on all of your devices after they have been installed.

Website settings can be synced across all devices, so just set them on one device and they'll be automatically set on all the others. Examples include Page Zoom, Request Desktop Website, Use Reader automatically, and more.

improved AVIF picture format support.

8. Notes:

The Lock Screen offers the option to quickly add a note.

Any app can make quick notes by using the share menu.

9. Contacts:

Now that duplicate contacts are automatically identified, users can merge them one at a time.

Individual fields can be chosen to only share them when exchanging contacts.

To better manage contacts, you can put them into different lists so you can quickly send emails to everyone on that list.

The ability to file contacts lists

10. Calendar:

Events can now be copied and pasted between the calendar's different days.

11. Files:

A user can change an image's format to JPEG, PNG, HEIF, and its size to Small, Medium, Large, or Original using a file's New Quick Actions.

12. Tips

The tipping UI has just been updated.

13. Books:

In order to improve the amount of space available for the contents and to make the pop-up panel easier to use when using the phone with one hand, the toolbar that formerly included the reading preferences, search, and bookmarks has been removed.

being able to change the text's line spacing, character spacing, word spacing, and full justification setting.

A new theme uses True Tone to automatically adapt the page colours based on the surrounding lighting.

14. Health:

The medications they take can be added to and managed by users.

Users can keep track of the sleep periods that the Apple Watch has identified.

15. Apple News:

New "My Sports" area with team-specific news, videos, and highlights. Users can utilise My Sports to add their favourite sports teams.

additional local news.

Group of New Favorites.

16. Weather:

New forecast modules that provide information on local forecasts, the condition of the air, etc.

10 day forecasts that include hourly forecasts and minute-by-minute precipitation intensity forecasts.

There are now interactive graphs that are more precise and simpler to interpret and that illustrate historical patterns in temperature, wind, humidity, etc.

Get alerts from the government when extreme weather occurs, such as tornadoes, winter storms, flash floods, etc.

19. Fitness:

Even if a user does not have an Apple Watch, they can now access the app.

20. Home:

Support has been added for the new global standard Matter for home automation.

21. iTunes TV:

With tvOS 16 and iOS 16, new experiences with Apple TV, Apple Watch, and iPhone are possible.

SECURITY AND PRIVACY:

1. Method of restraint:

Lockdown mode is a unique mode that, when activated, elevates security to the greatest level possible by limiting some functionalities of the OS, apps, and web platform in order to protect users from the most uncommon and sophisticated assaults.

Lockdown mode is viewed as a "extreme, optional mode that is not intended to be activated by the majority of users," in contrast to many other security measures. Instead, it is intended to serve as a defence against sophisticated malware and mercenary spyware, such as click less exploits or zero-click attacks, which are frequently hyper-targeted at influential people like journalists, diplomats, politicians, activists, lawyers, and well-known business figures.

2. Pass Keys:

The user can sign in to services that support WebAuthn across all of their devices without using a password thanks to Passkeys. Passwords are generated by the phone, and authorization is obtained using Touch ID or Face ID. Since pass keys employ AutoFill and Face ID or Touch ID for biometric authentication, Apple also makes sense of that.

3. Check for Safety:

This part of security resets all the given access and permissions to the people, apps and many other devices purposely for the iCloud account which is activated and this is also designed to help those people who are in abusive relationships.

4. Quick Security Reaction:

Today, significant OS updates are no longer necessary to deploy important security patches.

5. Increased clipboard security:

The ability to copy from the clipboard is currently restricted in several programmes and websites.

6. Tokens of Private Access:

In place of CAPTCHAs, a new technology called Private Access Tokens makes it possible to identify HTTP requests from trusted devices and individuals without jeopardizing their identity or personal information.

7. Message Identification Brand Indicators:

By placing the brand's emblem next to the email's header, Brand Indicators for Message Identification (BIMI) enables users to quickly identify verified emails sent by businesses.

HOW TO ACTIVATE ESIM TO IPHONE 14:

You must understand how to activate eSIM on iPhone 14 if you recently purchased a new iPhone. Regular SIM cards and eSIMs both perform comparable tasks. But since it is integrated inside the smartphone, you won't need to deal with a real nano SIM card. A new SIM card usage method is called eSIM. Since there is no actual SIM card involved, many people believe it to be more convenient. However, a large portion of people also believe that using eSIM is challenging. Since there are numerous activation stages, it is not as simple as the physical SIM. But do not fret. You can quickly activate eSIM on your iPhone using the advice in this post.

Steps to activate eSim on IPHONE 14:

Today's smartphones and tablets increasingly use eSIM. The iPhone often comes pre-loaded with an eSIM. While there is nothing you need to put inside the phone, you might need to install a new operator profile and configure the eSIM before using it. There are a few solutions available for activating the eSIM on your iPhone. Check to see if your carrier accepts eSIM.

- Embrace QR codes
- Scan the QR code provided by your carrier using the camera app that is open.
- When the notification for "Cellular Plan Detected" displays, tap it.
- To continue, click.

- To add a cellular plan, click.
- To activate the eSIM, enter the confirmation code given to you by the carrier.
- Install a carrier app
- Get the app for your carrier from the app store.
- Open the app, then use it to buy a cellular plan.

Steps to transfer or convert sim into eSim:

You can surely transfer your existing eSIM to your new iPhone if you already have one. There is also a simple method for converting a physical SIM to an eSIM if you already have one. Whatever you require, technology will give it to you.

- **When performing the Quick Start Setup on a new iPhone, add an eSIM card**.
- Select the phone number you want to use with your new iPhone during Quick Start setup.
- To proceed, simply tap the Continue button.
- **After setup, change a physical SIM or transfer an eSIM to a new iPhone.**
- On your new iPhone, launch the Settings app. After that, select Add Cellular Plan by tapping Cellular.
- Elect the Convert Cellular Plan option.
- Decide on Convert to eSIM.
- When a warning about an eSIM transfer displays, tap OK.
- Grab your previous iPhone, then select Transfer.
- Wait until the activation is complete.
- **On the same iPhone, change a physical SIM to an electronic SIM.**
- after selecting Settings, choose Cellular.
- Choose the eSIM button.

- Elect the Convert Cellular Plan option.
- Decide on Convert to eSIM.

The advantages of activating your eSIM far outweigh the adjustment period. The eSIM is really simpler to use than the traditional physical SIM card once you get the hang of it. All you need to know is how to transfer and convert a SIM card to an eSIM, as well as how to activate eSIM on your iPhone 14.

HOW TO CHANGE CAMERA SETTINGS:

The topic of how to change iPhone camera resolution settings is one that almost all iOS users have. The causes of it for every user. To alter camera settings for images or videos depending on the intended use, such as sharing, printing, copying, or uploading a low-resolution image if your phone's storage is limited. In this article, I provide the best, trickiest method for using the iPhone camera to capture images and videos with the highest possible resolution.

To achieve the best picture resolution on your iPhone without editing on a Mac or PC, use the solutions and techniques listed below:

Can iPhone images be converted to high resolution?

Remember that you must take a fresh photo using the high-resolution setting (steps mentioned below in this chapter). In other words, you can lower a photo's resolution but not raise it.

Change the iPhone 14 Pro Max's video resolution format.

On the iPhone 14 Series model, the user can adjust the video resolution within the camera app without touching the Settings app, negating the need to go the Settings app to do so. Let's look at the first steps.

- Step 1: Open the Camera app in Step 1
- Step2: Swipe the right side to reveal the screen for capturing videos.

- Step3: At this point, the resolution setting is shown in the screen's upper right-hand corner.
- Step4: Tap on it to change the recording format for the video resolution. [Tap 30 to switch to 60, and tap HD to switch to 4K video resolution setting]
- Step5: Then click or tap the red shutter icon to begin recording a video.

There is an option to record camera resolution for video only in the iPhone 14 Pro Max camera settings.

- Go to Settings > Camera. Select the only Camera option.
- Next, select a resolution, such as 4K.

Enjoy taking videos now at the resolution of your choosing. adjacent to the image. There is no need for higher resolution given the amazing results of the new iPhone 14 rear camera. Even so, you should check out the pro features app on the App Store, which is also helpful for creating low-resolution images that can be saved to the iPhone camera roll. Improved Portrait mode camera results are included with new iPhone models and the most recent iOS.

Picture Size:

A great app for moving your image into a specific resolution in terms of inches, pixels, millimeters, and centimetres is Image Size. The email should then be forwarded to you or saved to your iOS device at that point. A fantastic programme for creating the ideal image resolution. Also useful is Resize.

IPhone photo resizing and cropping:

iPhone photo resizing and cropping If you wish to resize or crop a picture accurately, you can do so without the use of a third-party app.

Another resolution-changing option is to reduce the image's size. To do this, open the pictures app, select a photo, then take a screenshot by simultaneously pressing the home and sleep/wake buttons. The original photo that was stored in your photographs app is too small compared to the size of your screenshot.

Extra Information:

A camera resolution settings software, which is the best low-resolution camera app available on the App Store, must be downloaded in order to capture a lower quality photo with your iPhone in various situations. To access the App Store, you must have an Apple ID and password.

HOW TO CHANGE PASSCODE ON IPHONE 14:

The best course of action to take when you have forgotten the passcode is explained in this chapter along with instructions on how to change the passcode on an iPhone 14 or other device. To unlock your cellphone using a method other than face ID or Touch ID, you must set up a lock screen password when setting up the device. You do want to alter it later, though. In this chapter we will give you a proper guide for changing of passcode.

How to change the passcode on an iPhone 14:

When you wish to change the passcode on an iPhone 14, follow these instructions:

- Go to Settings on your smartphone.
- Depending on the iOS version on your device, choose Passcode, Face ID, Passcode, or Touch ID, respectively.
- Type in the current passcode.
- Hit the Change Passcode button.
- Use the previous passcode.
- You must now input the fresh passcode. To choose amongst the several code types, tap Passcode Options.
- Once more, enter the new passcode.
- Wait for little than the passcode on your smartphone will be updated automatically.

HOW TO CHANGE 4-DIGIT PASSCODE ON IPHONE 14:

You still have the choice to use a four-digit passcode on your device, but you'll need to uncover the hidden settings to do so. We advise using a more complex passcode by following the procedures below because using four-digit passcodes is insufficiently safe.

- Go to Settings on your smartphone.
- Depending on the iOS version on your smartphone, tap Passcode, Face ID & Passcode, Touch ID & Passcode.
- Choose Change Passcode.
- Use the previous passcode.
- Hit the Passcode Options button. You will see alternatives as well.
- On the 4-Digit Numeric Code, tap.
- Type in the new passcode.
- For the second time, enter the new passcode.
- Instead of a lengthy passcode, you now have a new passcode with a four-digit numeric code.

HOW TO CHANGE PASSWORD ON IPHONE 14:

It is also feasible to use a passcode that consists of a mix of numbers and letters. Here are the steps to take and things to try on your iPhone 14:

- Click Settings on your iPhone 14 (iOS 16).
- Depending on the iOS version, tap Passcode, Face ID & Passcode, or Touch ID & Passcode.
- Put in the passcode.
- Choose Change Passcode.
- Use the previous passcode.
- Hit the Passcode Options button.
- Press the Custom Alphanumeric Code button.
- By using a combination of letters and digits, enter the new passcode.
- Once more, enter the new passcode.
- You have now created a new passcode using a combination of letters and digits, replacing the old one.

WHY YOU CAN'T CHANGE PASSWORD ON IPHONE 14:

This concludes the entire guide for changing the passcode on an iPhone 14. There are a few reasons why you can't modify it, like those listed below:

The passcode you typed is incorrect. To enter the proper passcode, lightly tap the keyboard.

You cannot remember the password. You cannot switch to a new passcode if you can't remember the current one.

Keep in mind that your device locks out if you input the wrong passcode six times in a row, but you can re-enter if you recall the passcode.

HOW TO USE SIRI ON IPHONE 14:

You can use Siri, an iOS digital assistant, to voice-control your iPhone. It is comparable to Amazon Alexa, which can be used to carry out any task on your smartphone. You can use it, for instance, to browse the internet, look up music, answer calls, and so many other things. We'll demonstrate how to use Siri to achieve the following things in this post.

- Modify Siri's voice it can be male/female
- Identify yourself to Siri
- Make use of the in-app shortcuts
- Ask Siri different questions
- Can read the incoming messages

HOW TO ACTIVATE SIRI ON IPHONE 14:

Step 1: You must first access the settings app.

Step 2: Now scroll down or search for Siri

Step 3: Now select the Press side button for Siri switch

Step 4: Now you have to select and Enable Siri to confirm

Step5: you have to make sure that you select Siri and allow when locked switch to enable or disable Siri on the lock screen.

Just that. By holding down the Side button until the Siri icon appears at the bottom of the screen, you can now ask Siri a question.

HOW TO CHANGE SIRI SOUND ON IPHONE 14:

Step 1: First, use the settings app.

Step 2: Scroll to and choose Siri & Search.

Step 3: Choose Siri Voice.

Depending on the nation and location, different voice genders are offered. Select Language from the Siri & Search screen to switch the language.

THINGS YOU CAN SAY TO SIRI :

1. There are numerous things you may ask Siri to do, including call, find contacts, obtain directions, set reminders and meetings, search the web, and identify songs. Asking Siri a lighthearted query like "What can you do for me?" will show you an example of what she is capable of on your device.

2. Siri can also perform translations on your behalf. Siri will translate a phrase that you speak in a foreign language, like Chinese or Italian, into that language.

3. When Siri is listening and processing your request, an audio orb will move at the bottom of the screen. Following that, a Siri dialogue will appear; choose the Siri to talk again.

HOW TO MAKE SIRI KNOW YOU?

To personalize your interactions with Siri, you'll need to make sure she knows and understands you very well. To do that, choose My information from the Siri Search page, then click on your Contact. Now that you know the answers, you may utilize them to find out things like "How do I go home?" and "What great restaurants are nearby."

HOW TO USE SIRI BUILT-IN APP SUPPORT:

One benefit of Siri is that it suggests shortcuts within apps and on the lock screen based on how you use them. If, for example, you open the same app every morning when you wake up, Siri will learn this and begin recommending it on the lock screen each morning for quick access.

Go to the Siri & Search page, go to the chosen app, and then click the desired option to turn on or off Siri suggestions. This will allow or disable Siri Suggestions on the Lock Screen or in-app suggestions.

HOW TO READ INCOMING MESSAGE USING SIRI:

You can ask Siri to read an incoming message on your iPhone through your Air Pods if you can't get to it. To achieve it, adhere to these procedures.

- Beginning with the settings on your smartphone.
- Decide on Notifications
- The third step is to choose Siri's Announce Messages.
- Lastly, in step four, click the Siri button for Announce Messages.
- The only Air Pods 2 or Power Beats Pro models that support this feature are required for use, and you can only do so while your iPhone is paired with them. Speaking to Siri allows you to reply to messages.
- Click the Send Replies Without Confirmation button to enable Siri to send messages without reading them to you first.

HOW TO TYPE INSTEAD OF SIRI SPEAKING:

Step 1: Select Siri under Settings > Accessibility.

Step 2: Enable Siri's Type feature.

Step 3: At this point, you can send Siri a message, ask her to perform a task for you, and utilize the keyboard and text field to communicate with her.

HOW TO USE PERSONAL INTERNET(HOTSPOT) FROM IPHONE 14:

You need to learn the proper technique for using Personal Hotspot on the iPhone 14 if you only need it temporarily. When your mobile device, laptop, or Mac cannot connect to the internet, a personal hotspot might be quite helpful.

When you wish to share the internet data on your device, a personal hotspot is helpful. It can be a device owned by you, a friend, or a family member. Additionally, if a member of your family requests it, you can create a password for a personal hotspot and connect it to your hotspot.

We will provide you with a detailed explanation of how to use the personal hotspot on your iPhone 14 running the most recent version of iOS in this chapter. Some updates in the most recent update are accessible under the personal hotspot's settings. The basic procedure is still exchanging data or connecting a new device to a personal hotspot, though.

Although the iPhone's personal hotspot is small, it is a helpful tool for connecting to the internet through Bluetooth or Wi-Fi when appropriate. It additionally requires a cellphone plan.

HOW TO USE PERSONAL HOTSPOT ON IPHONE 14:

When Wi-Fi network access is not available, you can share your iPhone 14's cellular data connection by using a personal hotspot.

Here are some quick instructions for using Personal Hotspot on an iPhone 14:

- Select Personal Hotspot under Settings.

- If Personal Hotspot isn't displayed here, tap Cellular to enable this option.

- If you still can't find it, check with your carrier to determine if your plan allows you to utilize Personal Hotspot.

- Your Personal Hotspot will instantly be listed in your network list when you connect one of your own devices that is logged into your iCloud account.

- Tap Allow Others to Join to let your friends and other devices join your connection.

- The Wi-Fi password for Your Personal Hotspot is also generated automatically, but you can tap it at any moment to alter it.

- Call your carrier if you can't find the personal hotspot option so you can utilise the Personal Hotspot with your plan.

HOW TO CONNECT PERSONAL HOTSPOT ON IPHONE 14:

The status bar glows blue when a new device is connected to your hotspot, as you can see. Additionally, it shows how many connected devices are there. The carrier and iPhone model determine how many devices can be simultaneously connected to your hotspot.

You must enter Settings, navigate to Cellular, and select Hotspot in order to connect a device to your hotspot. As an alternative, select Settings, look for Personal hotspot, and turn it on.

The Wi-Fi password and the device name must then be double checked. Keep your eyes on the screen until the other device has joined to the available Wi-Fi network.

Go to Settings and then select Wi-Fi to connect a device. On the list, you can search for your iPhone 14. Then, tap the Wi-Fi network to begin connecting to the network. You must input the personal hotspot password if necessary.

HOW TO RESTORE FILE AND BACKUP:

You have backed up precious information on iCloud, and now you want to restore it easily and without encountering any issues. Then you should read this chapter. People back up large data so they can quickly access them when they purchase a new mobile device or reset their old one. However, the issue occurs during the restoration process because it is rife with difficulties and hiccups.

But fortunately for you, I'll be explaining how to achieve this quickly. So, how can you quickly recover your iPhone 14 from an iCloud backup? For more information, keep reading. Let's begin!

Every person's mobile device contains some valuable data (photos, movies, and papers) that are too priceless to be lost or erased. Because of this, they back it up so that everything may still be restored even if they had to erase it temporarily.

Particularly for iPhone owners, backing up their data to iCloud and restoring it after a factory reset or new device purchase is simple. Additionally, restoring a new iPhone from an iCloud backup is really simple. Inquiring as to how?

Follow these steps to restore your iPhone from an iCloud backup:

- Your new iPhone 14 should be turned on before choosing settings like language and region.
- Next, select "App and Data" from the menu and tap on "SET UP MANUALLY"

- The restoration process will then start after your login in with your Apple ID on your iPhone 14 and tap "Restore from iCloud Backup.
- So, there you have it—how to restore an iPhone from an iCloud backup.

This approach, however, has a drawback. There is a problem if you wish to recover data while using an iPhone 14 that you have already purchased. After backing up your data to iCloud, you must reset your phone to be able to access it. The loss of any crucial data that you might have forgotten to back up could result from doing this. Moreover, whenever you use iCloud for data backup and restoration, storage issues inevitably arise. It is therefore not that straightforward to restore an iPhone from an iCloud backup.

Therefore, it's imperative that you only use techniques or solutions that remove your restrictions and fear of data loss. But there's a way to make this problem solved.

RESTORE IPHONE 14 DATA BY TOOL:

When you attempt to restore the data, many issues could occur. These may potentially have an adverse effect on the device or result in permanent data loss. Fortunately, there is a solution you may use to restore the data from your iPhone 14 without any restrictions. It's Tenorshare iCareFone, a dependable programme with excellent outcomes.

One of the greatest data backup and restoration tools is iCareFone, which can be used with both iOS and Android devices. The interface is simple to use, backing up and restoring data happens quickly, and most importantly, it is secure.

Tenor share iCareFone data backup and restoration instructions are as follows:

- On your Mac or PC, download and install it before launching it. Connect your iPhone 14 to a computer via a USB cable next. To begin the data recovery procedure, click "Backup and Restore."

- Every file that has been backed up will be displayed on the screen when you click Restore on the left side of the screen. By selecting the "View" option at the bottom, you may also view a preview of these files.

- When you select the files you wish to restore, the system might prompt you for your password for security reasons. After selecting the files, click on the Restore or Export option, and the contents will be quickly restored and saved.

Please be aware that iCareFone only offers direct device restoration of images, movies, music, contacts, and bookmarks.

FAQS ABOUT ICLOUD BACKUP:

1. Can I delete my iCloud backup? Will the iPhone be properly erased?

The iCloud backup can be removed without affecting your device. However, as it will be permanently deleted from the iCloud storage, you won't be able to retrieve it any more. Additionally, this will disable iCloud backup.

Keep in mind that removing an iCloud backup won't remove all content from the mobile device. Only the data that was backed up will be deleted.

2. How to View and Delete Previous iPhone iCloud Backups?

People regularly need to view and erase old data in order to make room for new data because there is only 5GB of storage available in iCloud. This is the procedure:

- Then touch on your name in Settings.
- Next, select "Manage Storage" from the list of options under "iCloud," where you'll find the "Backup" option. Touch it.

SUMMARY OF BACKING UP:

How then can the iPhone 14 be restored from an iCloud backup?

After you set up the region and settings of the new or factory reset device, go to App & Data and follow the simple instructions to restore iCloud-backed data. However, issues can arise throughout this process, and the restoration process occasionally fails.

You should seek assistance from the best software, such as Tenorshare iCareFone, to restore data without any restrictions. It is quick, secure, dependable, and simple to use. Data backup and restoration are quick, simple processes. It has been used by thousands of people, all of whom have nothing but positive things to say about it.

Download Tenorshare iCareFone to easily restore all of your data.

HOW TO SCAN TEXT INTO IPHONE NOTES VERSION 14:

If your iPhone 14 is compatible with the iOS 15.4 operating system, you can scan text into notes using that device. This capability is available to users of the iPad 15.4 operating system as well. Apple made the world aware of this functionality in March 2022.

You may rapidly enter printed or even handwritten text into the Notes app on your iPhone or iPad by using the "Scan Text" shortcut.

Here is a guide on how to use the camera to scan text or documents into the Notes app:

Text into Notes using Scan:

Using the camera, you can use this capability to insert scanned text. Please be aware that it is only for supported languages and supported models running iOS 15.4 or later. Here are the steps to try if you wish to scan text into notes on an iPhone 14:

- Click the camera symbol in a note, then select Scan Text.
- Position your smartphone such that the text is visible in the camera's field of view.
- When you tap on the text icon, you will see the yellow frame that helps you read the text.
- You can either drag or use the grab points to select the text. Tap insert just after that.

HOW TO SCAN A DOCUMENT:

The steps to scanning a document into Notes are as follows:

- Find the camera icon in a note by opening the note apps. Select Scan Documents after that.
- Placing the iPhone will allow you to see the document page on the screen. iPhone will immediately capture the page. Tap on the shutter button to manually capture the page. Alternately, you can use the iPhone 14's volume button. The thunder icon can be found when you see the camera. This symbol makes it simple to toggle on or off the flash.
- Continue scanning pages, and when you're finished, tap Save.
- You now have the documents that were saved. Some editing features, including adding more pages, cropping, applying a filter, rotating, marking up the document, or erasing the scan, may be useful.

In order to scan text into the Notes application on older versions of iOS 15 and iPad 15, you must first tap the text field for the note and then tap the Live Text icon.

Other new features from Apple include Universal Control on compatible iPad models, more new emojis, and the new voice option on Siri, as well as the ability to unlock the iPhone using the updated facial ID technology without removing your mask.

CLEANING TIPS:

Ordinarily harmless dust and scratches won't harm your priceless equipment until they do. Without proper control, these two unwelcome items will soon ruin your investment by obscuring their lustrous appearances or eating away at the protective films covering those electronics.

Let me now bring the entire discussion home. The optics on your iPhone 14 Pro/Max are slightly more exposed and have a slightly broader field of view than its forerunners. The microscopic dust particles that are constantly floating around will eventually gather on the surface in a few days, even if you store it in the cleanest of spaces. Additionally, accumulated dust can dramatically reduce the effectiveness of your iPhone camera if you don't practice good cleaning habits. For instance, dust's effect is more harmful the more surfaces it contacts. When there are tiny particles of dust all over your camera, the image quality may suffer and the lens may eventually become damaged. The screen operates similarly. Dust can significantly scratch the screen, reducing its visibility if it is not regulated. Many choose Camera Protectors for iPhone 14 Pro/14 Pro Max right away.

Some general safety measures you can implement to safeguard your investment are:

Keep your keys and iPhone 14 Pro Max apart.

People frequently keep their phones and many keys in the same pocket. That is an efficient technique to note some noticeable screen scratches on the phone! Additionally, some keys even have the potential to dent the camera lens or screen. Therefore, always carry these two items apart.

Ensure That Your iPhone 14 Pro Max Is Sitting On a Flat, Stable Surface.

Keeping your priceless iPhone 14 Pro/Pro Max on a slick surface increases the likelihood that it may fall off. This safety measure may seem obvious and commonsense, yet many iPhone owners have lost their devices because they kept them on a surface that was unsteady. So, avoid taking the chance.

Purchase camera protection

Installing a camera protector is a more practical approach to protect your iPhone 14 Pro/14 Pro Max. In this manner, even if it were to fall, the protector would likely be the only component to be affected. You can easily take it out and put a new one. Additionally, dust is easily removed off the protection with a clean cloth. Screen protectors also function in this way to prevent regret.

Some of the affordable glass lens protector are:

- Tempered Glass Lens protector
- Classic kickstand case

Tempered Glass Lens protector:

This item offers a cutting-edge method for safeguarding the powerful camera engine of your iPhone 14 Pro or Pro Max. It's unique to these two iPhone 14 models and won't function on any other iPhone. The photographs you would have obtained without using your iPhone 14 Pro Max are just as good, bright, and clear with the lens protector present.

These camera lens shields are not only ultra-clear but also slender and light in weight.

You get this lens protection from tempered glass, which is famed for its strength. If your iPhone falls, you can be sure that the lens will be protected by a strong first-layer shield.

Features of using this protector:

- Crystal clear
- Complete installation kit
- Perfect fit for your phone
- Tempered too tough
- Mainly scratch resistant

Classic kickstand case:

The metal kickstand located around the camera portion of this hybrid case shields the lens of your iPhone 14 Pro Max. The kickstand creates a bezel around the area even when it is not in use, keeping your lens from rubbing against objects. Protection for the body and screen of this Apple flagship is provided by the case itself. Therefore, if you purchase it, you will have peace of mind knowing that nothing seriously dangerous will get in contact with your camera lens.

The metal kickstand is rust-resistant zin-alloy and is particular good or service up to 80 degrees. Every part of your iPhone 14 Pro Max fits exactly into its designated areas in this case, and all corners are shock-absorbing due to being air-guarded. This iPhone 14 Pro Classic Kickstand Case provides the same level of protection for your phone's camera lens and screen as described above if you have an iPhone 14 Pro.

The main difference between the two is that while the first one is compatible with the iPhone 14 Pro Max, the second is only available for the iPhone 14 Pro. They guarantee that your gadget is sturdy and scratch- and dust-resistant.

Features of using this protector:

- Camera guard kickstand
- Premium material
- Hybrid clear case
- Military grade protection

It is cheaper to prevent accidents and damages on pricey devices like the iPhone 14 Pro / Max than to try to repair them. You may use your Apple smartphone with confidence for a very long time if you take the precautions advised in this book and implement the suggested items to assist solve some frequent security problems.

HOW TO TAKE SCREENSHOT:

If you're wondering how to screenshot on iPhone 14, it's simple. How to take a screenshot involves capturing any visuals that are displayed on your device's screen. You will find detailed instructions in this book that apply to the iPhone 14, iPhone 14 Pro, and iPhone 14 Pro Max as well.

BEST METHODS TO TAKE SCREEN SHOT:

Using the two buttons on either side of the iPhone 14 is the simplest way to snap a screenshot. Press the Side button and the Volume Up button together for a brief moment to begin employing this technique (located on the right side). This procedure must be applied simultaneously.

Although pressing both buttons simultaneously can be a little difficult, you can manage it and a shutter sound effect will result (Just make sure that your device volume is not muted). A thumbnail of the screenshot you just took will appear in the lower-left corner of your device's screen later.

Due to your disregard for the screenshot's thumbnail, it will eventually vanish. If not, simply swipe it away to delete the screenshot. Your iPhone 14 will immediately store this screenshot to your Photos app after the thumbnail vanishes. However, as of December 2021, no user has the option to turn off the thumbnail preview, albeit it can be altered in the newest version of iOS.

EDIT SCREEN SHOT:

Therefore, in this step, we'll presume that you can see the thumbnail that appears in the bottom-right corner of your device's screen after taking a screenshot. The editing mode will then appear when you tap it. Before saving the image, you can use this method to crop, rotate, and perform other editing operations.

If you are unhappy with the outcome, you can also remove the screenshot. Simply tap the trash symbol in the top-right corner of your device's screen to accomplish this. When you are finished in edit mode, you must hit "Done" after seeing the corner of the screen. You can choose "Save to Photos" to proceed. Your updated screenshot will be immediately saved to the Photos app on your smartphone at this point.

CAPTURE A SCREEN SHOT WITH BACKTOP:

The detailed methods for taking a screenshot on the iPhone 14 utilizing the Back Tap feature The ideal approach is this one if you consistently have issues pressing the buttons to snap screenshots.

You can benefit from a feature called "Back Tap." You must attach tape to the back of your gadget. Simply configure it by going to "Settings" and then selecting "Accessibility."

You must tap "Touch" and select "Back Tap" from the menu here. Assign "Screenshot" to the double- or triple-tap option to continue the procedure. Once you've done that, your device will let you take a screenshot by tapping the iPhone's back.

HOW TO SETUP VOICEMAIL ON IPHONE 14:

Similar to the previous iPhone and other iOS devices, setting up voicemail on the iPhone 14 only requires a few straightforward steps.

GUIDE TO SET UP:

To get started, launch the Phone app and select Voicemail. Afterward, select Set Up Now. It's important to understand that your voicemail requires a password. Decide on it, then select the greeting you like.

HOW TO CHECK VOICEMAIL:

It's important to check your voicemail after setting it up on your iPhone 14 by following the steps above. On this gadget, checking voicemail is a cinch. It is equivalent to going to the Phone app and selecting the Voicemail option. Visual Voicemail, which is available on all iPhone models, allows you to view the list of voicemails. However, not all carriers, regions, or languages have access to the service or voicemail transcription. Thus, it depends on your circumstances. Even if your smartphone lacks these features, it is still doable.

Select Voicemail after opening the Phone App. Tap the play button after selecting the message you want to hear from your voicemail.

If you want to send a message to the Deleted Messages folder, select the delete option. From here, you can either permanently delete or undelete the message. Once more, it varies by nations and areas because on some particular carriers, the providers are allowed to delete the texts.

In the unlikely event that your iPhone 14 does not support the Visual Voicemail feature, you must first open the Voicemail and then adhere to the screen's instructions. If you wish to access the voicemail, you can do so by using Siri. Say "Play a voicemail from a specific individual" once Siri is active. Siri will play the voicemail in accordance with your request.

TIP AND TRICKS FOR USING VOICE MAIL:

It is possible to modify the settings once voicemail has been configured on the iPhone 14. Open the voicemail to get started. Tap on Greeting after that. Here, you will alter your welcome. To alter the voicemail password, however, open the Settings menu, choose Phone, and then touch on Change Voicemail Password. The new voicemail password can be entered here.

Under the unlikely event that you want to alter the voicemail alert, you must first locate Sound & Haptics in Settings. As an alternative, you can get to it by going to Settings and selecting Sounds. The voicemail alert sound should then be customized to your exact specifications.

It's fantastic to be able to tap on a message in Voicemail and see the transcription if your device supports voicemail transcription. For your knowledge, transcription is now in beta, thus it's conceivable that there will be technical issues. The caliber of the recorded message is another factor in transcription. As a result, each user's experience with this feature will be unique.

HOW TO USE FACETIME HANDOFF:

Precautions when using FaceTime Handoff

- Only Apple devices with the same Apple ID can use FaceTime Handoff.
- To use FaceTime Handoff, your devices must be running macOS Ventura, iOS 16, and iPadOS 16 or later.
- Make sure to join the same Wi-Fi network with both devices.

More capabilities have recently been added to FaceTime as part of Apple's effort to make it the greatest video calling service available. FaceTime is quickly catching up to the many built-in apps that now have new iOS 16 functionality. The app offers a few really great new features, but Handoff particularly struck my eye.

It's useful to have the option of hassle-free call transfer between Apple devices. Even more so if you are someone who uses several gadgets at once. You don't need to switch smartphones and end the FaceTime call; you can just transfer devices with a few clicks.

Activating FaceTime Handoff:

Even though FaceTime Handoff is set to be enabled by default, it is still a good idea to check. However, you should be aware that FaceTime Handoff is only compatible with iPhones running iOS 16 or later, iPads using iPadOS 16, and Macs using macOS Ventura.

Now that you have performed the essential checks, let's see how to activate this practical feature.

ON IPHONE 14:

- Open settings on your iphone and tap on genera
- Now tap air play and handoff
- Now simply toggle on Handoff

FACETIME:

This time analyst Ming-Chi Kuo is delivering some excellent facts regarding the front-facing camera, which will experience a nice improvement after two years without being fully updated. Usually, we hear a lot about the main sensor on the iPhone 14 series.

The analyst predicts that all four iPhone 14 models will probably get an upgrade with autofocus and a bigger aperture.

In comparison to the iPhone 13's FF (fixed-focus) and f/2.2 aperture, the front cameras of the four new iPhone 14 models in 2H22 are likely to be upgraded to AF (autofocus) and roughly f/1.9. For selfie/portrait mode, AF support and a lower f-number can produce a shallower depth-of-field effect. Additionally, the focus impact for FaceTime, video calls, and live streaming can be improved by AF.

The Portrait and Cinematic modes would benefit greatly from these modifications. Additionally, low-light selfies might benefit from a nice improvement. According to the analyst, this could also improve the focus effect for FaceTime, video calls, and live streaming applications.

It's crucial to note how much Apple concentrated on FaceTime capabilities during the previous WWDC, thus implementing this improvement at this time would make a lot of sense for the iPhone 14 series. The iPhone 14 Pro models will most likely have a new look with a hole punch + pill design in addition to that, while the normal models will still have the iPhone 13 notch.

HOW TO SET UP AND USE BACK TOP ON IPHONE 14:

Not everyone is familiar with the iPhone 14's Back Tap feature. Apple always knows how to deliver the best surprise in its products for its users, even if you are a new Apple user and own the newest or best iPhones.

You can try to locate the hidden feature in the Settings app if you're a new iPhone 14 owner. Similar to Google's Quick Tap function, which was originally made available on the Pixel 5 as part of the Android 12 update, this feature is also available on Pixel phones.

SETTING UP BACK TAP:

Although it is comparable to the Quick Tap feature, the Apple version is more adaptable. Unlike the Android solution, which only supports double-taps, this one allows for multiple taps. Apple, though, goes beyond that. Your device's back can be triple-tapped to start an application, scroll left or right, and turn on the torch.

Back Tap is the name of the feature on the iPhone 14. You can modify how you use this gadget by using this feature. This article explains how to enable and use back tap on the iPhone 14 and open up a world of fresh possibilities.

- Go to the Settings application.
- After you scroll down, tap Accessibility.
- Click Touch.
- Find Back Tap at the bottom of the page, then tap on it.

- Double tap and triple tap are available. One or both of those options can be activated. Tap "None" next to the choice you want to choose to do this.

-

- The list of options is what you will see next. After choosing one, tap it so a checkmark is displayed next to it, and then tap again to set this feature.

To choose from, your device will provide a few possibilities. It can be used to start the camera, access the control panel, or display the notification center. Even you can use this function to take a screenshot, adjust the volume, and return to the Home screen.

Go to Settings > Accessibility > Touch > Back Touch, select Double Tap or Triple Tap, then tap None to disable Back tap.

WHAT CAN THIS FEATURE DO?

By double-tapping on the rear of your iPhone 14, for instance, you can utilise this feature to set scroll up if you enjoy reading books on the device. Alternately, by triple tapping on the back, you can read lengthy text with one hand. You can perform a lot of things by configuring your device's back tap feature, though.

Depending on the option you chose, double- or triple-tap the rear of your smartphone to test it out and see how it functions. However, keep in mind that in order to use Back Tap on iPhone 14, your device must be compatible with iOS

14 or higher. That's all there is to it for enabling Back Tap on your smartphone.

HOW TO USE FOCUS ON IPHONE 14:

By reducing distractions, the focus feature aids in improving concentration. Additionally, it will assist you in automatically filtering applications and notifications on your phone according to your status. It is significant since employing this tool can help you cut down on distractions. Let's read the whole guide below if you want to use the focus on the iPhone 14.

Additionally, this function enables you to set your phone to a specific Focus, such as Work, Personal, Gaming, Sleep, or Exercising, and your smartphone can automatically hide distractions while filtering all notifications and informing your friends that you are unavailable. A focus feature must be activated directly in the Control Center in order to be used. As an alternative, you must schedule it to activate automatically. Here is a detailed user manual for Focus on iPhone 14:

- Navigate to Control Center, then select Focus. Tap the Focus again to make it active after that. For instance, select Do Not Disturb. You must switch to the new Focus if another one is already active.
- To select an ending for this feature, tap the three dots. Select the option after that. For instance, until I leave this spot, or you might choose for an hour. Tap the three dots once more after that.
- The status bar will display the feature's icon after you enable it. You will, for instance, see the half-moon symbol for the "Do Not Disturb" focus function. It will also be visible on the device's lock screen. Therefore, the

smartphone will immediately display the status in the Messages app. If a friend tries to message you, they will notice that you have disabled notifications, but they can still let you know if something essential has happened. By selecting Focus from the Settings menu after touching on it, you can switch a Focus on or off. Set the Focus function to on.

HOW TO USE SIRI TO ENABLE AND DISABLE FOCUS:

Using Siri, you, as the user, can turn on or off a Focus. You can accomplish this by tapping on the microphone or Siri symbol and then saying something like "Turn on the Work Focus" or "Turn off the Work Focus."

Once you've finished using a Focus, you may easily turn it off to enable alerts. A Focus that has been disabled is still available for use in Control Center. The steps to disabling focus on iPhone 14 are as follows:

- On your device's Lock Screen, tap and hold the Focus symbol. You can also launch Control Center as an alternative. Tap Focus after that.
- To turn off the Focus, simply tap on it.

You can, however, delete a Focus if you decide you no longer need it. The steps are as follows:

- Navigate to Settings, then select Focus.
- Scroll to the bottom of the screen after tapping on the Focus. You can then select Delete Focus. You must re-configure a Focus by going to Settings, finding it there, and selecting + if you wish to delete it.

That concludes the instruction on how to utilize Focus on an iPhone 14 as well as how to activate it through Siri and uninstall it.

HOW TO INSERT MEDICAL ID ON IPHONE 14:

You must understand how to set up Medical ID on an iPhone 14 if you own one. When you are in a dire situation and require medical attention, this fantastic function can literally save your life. Unexpected medical emergencies can occur. You must utiliZe the life-saving capability that your iPhone 14 has supplied. The following information will help you set up a Medical ID on your iPhone 14.

First responders can use Medical ID to retrieve vital details about your health right from your phone. In order for the medical staff to know who to call when you are in an emergency, you can also set an emergency contact. The Medical ID is simple to set up. Simply carry out the following actions:

- On your iPhone 14, launch the Health app.
- Summary of tap.
- Tap the symbol for your profile photo. On your phone, it is in the upper right corner.
- Toggle Medical ID.
- Select Edit.
- Enter your medical information, including your blood type, height, weight, date of birth, allergies, responses, and medical conditions. Don't leave anything out to give the first responders as much information as possible about you.
- Additionally, you can list who to contact in case of emergency. Simply select the contact you want, and then indicate how you feel about them.

- When you reach the Emergency Access area, scroll to the bottom of the screen. Your medical information can be viewed even while your iPhone 14 is locked if the Show When Locked feature is enabled. By selecting Medical ID under Emergency on your iPhone 14, first responders will be able to access this.

REASONS TO SETUP MEDICAL ID:

Understanding how to configure Medical ID on the iPhone 14 is crucial. You can assist your parents or other family members in setting up this function if they have particular medical conditions so they can receive the right care in the event of an emergency. Here are a few more justifications for using this functionality.

Setting up emergency contact:

Understanding how to configure Medical ID on the iPhone 14 is crucial. You can assist your parents or other family members in setting up this function if they have particular medical conditions so they can receive the right care in the event of an emergency. Here are a few more justifications for using this functionality.

Easy access:

It's become obsolete to record your medical information on paper. The easiest way for medical staff to learn about your medical condition is through Medical ID on your iPhone 14. The good news is that even when your phone is locked, Medical ID can still be accessed. When the iPhone 14 is locked, first responders can access Medical ID by selecting Medical ID after hitting Emergency on the Lock Screen.

When someone is experiencing a medical emergency, every second counts. This is why every iPhone user needs a Medical ID. You should enable Medical ID on your iPhone 14 and make sure all of your information is entered completely so that it can be used in an emergency.

HOW TO TRANSFER DATA FROM IPHONE TO IPHONE:

Whether you recently upgraded to one of the best iPhones or received an older device as a gift, understanding how to transfer data from iPhone to iPhone will certainly be the first item on your list. The logical initial action after turning on your iPhone is to transfer data from one iPhone to another. Apple is completely aware of this and has therefore created a variety of options to transfer data between iPhones, including wirelessly through iCloud and using a PC.

Additionally, if you're using iOS 15, a new procedure offers free iCloud temporary storage space, greatly streamlining the process. You're prepared to move data from one iPhone to another. Check out the many techniques in our guide below.

Apple developed a feature that enables data transfer from iPhone to iPhone even simpler with iOS 16. To make the process as simple as possible, it's called Prepare for New iPhone and offers free temporary storage space in iCloud for 21 days.

TRANSFER:

- This avoids having to pay for additional storage as long as you transfer your data to your new iPhone within 21 days after initiating the process. You can apply for an additional 21 days if you think it is not long enough.
- First, select General under Settings. Next, scroll to the screen's bottom and select Transfer or Reset iPhone.

- At the top of the screen, you'll find the Prepare for New iPhone function. Select Get Started.
- Tap Continue once you've finished reading the material.
- Then, you could be prompted to select Turn on Backup to Transfer (unless iCloud Backup is already turned on). After choosing Move All App Data using iCloud, click Done. Data and applications will begin to upload to iCloud. On the main Settings page, you can monitor the backup status.

HOW TO TRANSFER USING ICLOUD:

Having a backup of your device can provide you piece of mind in the event that your iPhone is ever lost or stolen, even if you are not wanting immediately, transfer data from one iPhone to another. The advantage is that you may store the data safely in iCloud and transfer it whenever you need to Start by launching the Settings app, choosing your name from the list at the top, and then choosing iCloud. Choose which apps to use iCloud by going through the list of services and making your decision. Tap a toggle or select On or Off depending on the options offered. Keep in mind that free iCloud accounts can only have 5GB of storage. Tap Manage Storage if you'd like more. You have the option to pay for 50GB, 200GB, or 2TB of storage after choosing Change Storage Plan. If you wish to back up your entire iPhone to iCloud, you will need to increase the amount of space you utilize.

- Automatic backups are a possibility Just tap iCloud Backup to turn it on. You can also immediately backup your iPhone to iCloud. Tap Back Up Now to accomplish this.

- You will have a sizable amount of data to transfer if you decide to switch from one iPhone to another.

- When your new iPhone (or one that has been deleted and reset) starts up, select your language and region, then press Set Up Manually on the Quick Start page. Following choosing a Wi-Fi network, tapping Next, and giving the iPhone a moment to activate.

- Things like Touch ID can be configured immediately or later. You'll arrive to the Apps & Data page once you've given your iPhone a passcode. You can select Restore from iCloud Backup here.

- Choose the most recent iCloud backup after logging up with your iCloud Apple ID. All you have to do is wait while the data is transferred to the new iPhone.

HOW TO TRANSFER USING QUICK START:

If you're putting up a new iPhone, there is an even simpler method of transferring data: Quick Start The quickest technique to move data to your new iPhone, it will briefly tie up both your new and old devices.

- Before anything else, power on the new iPhone and set the previous one next to it. A popup to "Set Up New iPhone" displays as you proceed. Click "Unlock" to proceed. The setup will be completed using the Apple ID associated with your old phone. Click Continue if you don't mind.

- On the screen of the new iPhone, there will be an animation Put the animation in front of the camera on your old iPhone. When you receive the "Finish on New

[Device]" notice, enter the passcode you use for your previous smartphone on your new iPhone and proceed with the setup instructions.

- Select Transmit Directly from iPhone and confirm the settings and data you wish to transfer when you arrive at the Transfer Your Data panel.

HOW TO TRANSFER USING WINDOWS PC:

Using your Windows computer, you can transfer data from one iPhone to another. Just make sure your PC has either a Type-C or normal USB port available, depending on the type of Lightning cable you're using. Download and install iTunes from the Microsoft Store first if you don't already have it on your computer (opens in new tab).

- Attach a Lightning cable to your old iPhone and your PC with the other end for data backup then open iTunes and choose Summary from the left-hand menu. Click Back Up Now after selecting This Computer in the Backups section.
- On the Quick Start page that appears when you launch your new iPhone, hit Set Up Manually. Follow the on-screen prompts until you click Restore from Mac or PC on the Apps & Data screen. Continue to adhere to the on-screen instructions to complete the process.

HOW TO TRANSFER USING MAC:

- First, launch the Finder application and choose your iPhone from the left-sidebar menu. Click Back up now and then select Back up all the data from your iPhone to your Mac.

- On the Quick Start page that appears when you launch a new iPhone, hit Set Up Manually. Follow the on-screen instructions until you click Restore from Mac or PC on the Apps & Data screen.

Knowing how to transfer data from one iPhone to another may make you curious to look at other iPhone instructions. Learn about the numerous capabilities in the Messages app by reading 15 vital suggestions for iPhone owners, then follow these instructions to update your iPhone to the newest version of iOS.

HOW TO TRANSFER DATA FROM ANDROID TO IPHONE 14:

The difficulties and failures that force the procedure to resume from the beginning will be the most annoying part of moving data from Android to iPhone 14. In order to avoid such situations, utilising a computer or a PC is recommended.

Method 1: After setup, use Mobile Trans to transfer Android to the iPhone 14.

Wonder share for cross-platform data transfer, such as from Android to iOS, Android to Android, iOS to iOS, and iOS to Android, Mobile Trans is an all-in-one solution. Compared to sharing or transferring files through Bluetooth or Wi-Fi, the software offers a faster data transfer. The best thing is that the data transfer from an Android device to the new iPhone 14 may be done without an internet connection.

Compatible Data Types

Mobile trans enables the transfer of contacts, voice memos, calendar events, movies, bookmarks, and media files from Android to iPhone.

Do you want to know how to set up Wonder share Mobile Trans and then transfer Android to an iPhone? Here is a detailed instruction:

- Open Wonder share Mobile Trans on your PC, then connect your new iPhone 14 and outdated Android device.
- Click the Phone to Phone button under the Phone Transfer tab.
- By choosing the data type and clicking the Start button, you can move that data from your old Android device to your new iPhone 14. Depending on the magnitude of the data, the operation should be finished in a few minutes.

Pros

- simple to use
- There is no requirement for technical knowledge.
- quickly and safely

Cons

Data transfer is restricted in the trial version.

Any Android device can now be upgraded to the new iPhone 14 without difficulty. Utilize Wonder share Mobile trans to quickly transfer all the data!

2nd Method: The second approach is to use iTunes to switch between an iPhone and an Android device.

Another practical method for transferring data from your Android device to the new iPhone 14 is via iTunes. To transfer content to an iPhone 14, though, you must first copy it from an Android device to a PC and then use the iTunes library to do so. Following is a step-by-step instruction sheet:

- Compatible data types
- Audio, video, and pictures
- Transfer music and photographs from your Android device to your PC by connecting the two.
- Open iTunes and join your new iPhone 14 to your PC using it.
- Now, navigate to File and select Add File to Library to add the files you copied from
- Following the addition of the files, select Music from the left menu and check the box next to "Entire music library, include videos and voice memos."

then select to use the same procedure to sync both photographs and videos on your iPhone 14.

Pros

- iTunes is a secure program.
- You can decide what information to send.

Cons

- Only 3–4 categories of data are supported.

Part 2: Using an iPhone or iPad without a PC to Transfer Data

If you don't have a PC or computer to move the info from Android to iPhone? No need to worry anymore! Without a PC, you can also exchange files across Android or iOS devices. The following techniques

The first method is called "Move to iOS with Move Data from Android to iPhone 14."

You can transfer data from Android to the iPhone 14 via Wi-Fi by switching to the iOS program. The Wi-Fi should be on, and the gadgets should be charged, among other considerations. How to transfer data from Android to iOS is shown below:

- Supportable data types
- other than music, books, and PDFs, all data kinds
- Choose the Move Data from Android option while activating the new iPhone 14.
- Activate the Move to iOS app on your Android phone. After choosing Continue, follow the on-screen instructions to complete the setup.
- You can find a code on the screen of your new iPhone 14. When using the Android version of the Move to iOS app, write down the code and enter it. on moving to iOS, type the code
- A temporary Wi-Fi network will be created by the new iPhone 14 device that your Android device must join. On your Android, a Transfer Data screen will show up after you connect to the network.

Transfer data from Android to iOS using Google Drive

- You may transfer files from Android to iOS using Google Drive, a cloud storage platform that is similar to Dropbox. Images, audio, video, and a variety of other types of data can all be stored on Google Drive, which provides 15GB of free storage.
- Supported data kinds

- Documents, contacts, calendar, SMS messages, pictures, and videos
- On your Android phone, launch the Google Drive app and sign in with your account information.
- Tap Menu, choose Backups, and then tap Backup now from the Google Drive app.
- On your iPhone 14, install Google Drive, then log in with the same Google account. To your iPhone 14, download the files.

Made in the USA
Monee, IL
28 November 2022

18862519R00066